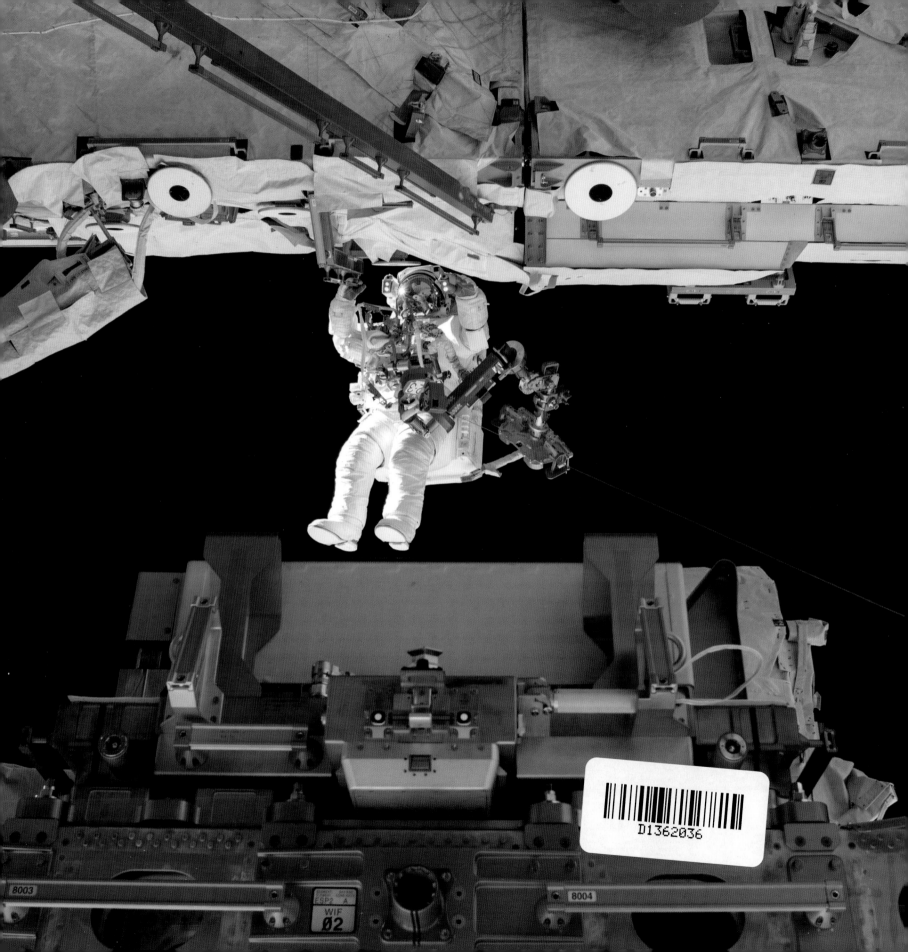

AMERICAN MUSEUM
ᵒᶠ NATURAL HISTORY

STERLING CHILDREN'S BOOKS
New York

An Imprint of Sterling Publishing Co., Inc.
1166 Avenue of the Americas
New York, NY 10036

ISBN 978-1-4549-2327-5

Distributed in Canada by Sterling Publishing Co., Inc.
c/o Canadian Manda Group, 664 Annette Street
Toronto, Ontario M6S 2C8, Canada
Distributed in the United Kingdom by GMC Distribution Services
Castle Place, 166 High Street, Lewes, East Sussex BN7 1XU, England
Distributed in Australia by NewSouth Books
45 Beach Street, Coogee, NSW 2034, Australia

For information about custom editions, special sales, and premium and corporate purchases,
please contact Sterling Special Sales at 800-805-5489 or specialsales@sterlingpublishing.com.

Manufactured in China

Lot #:
2 4 6 8 10 9 7 5 3 1
11/17

sterlingpublishing.com

All photos from NASA except:
Alamy: © ITAR-TASS Photo Agency: 9 (left)
Courtesy of the American Museum of Natural History: 28
iStock: © hudienm: throughout (graph paper); © Natalia_80: throughout (stars)

Cover and interior design by Irene Vandervoort

American Museum ᵒᶠ Natural History

LIFE IN SPACE

Ben Richmond

STERLING CHILDREN'S BOOKS
New York

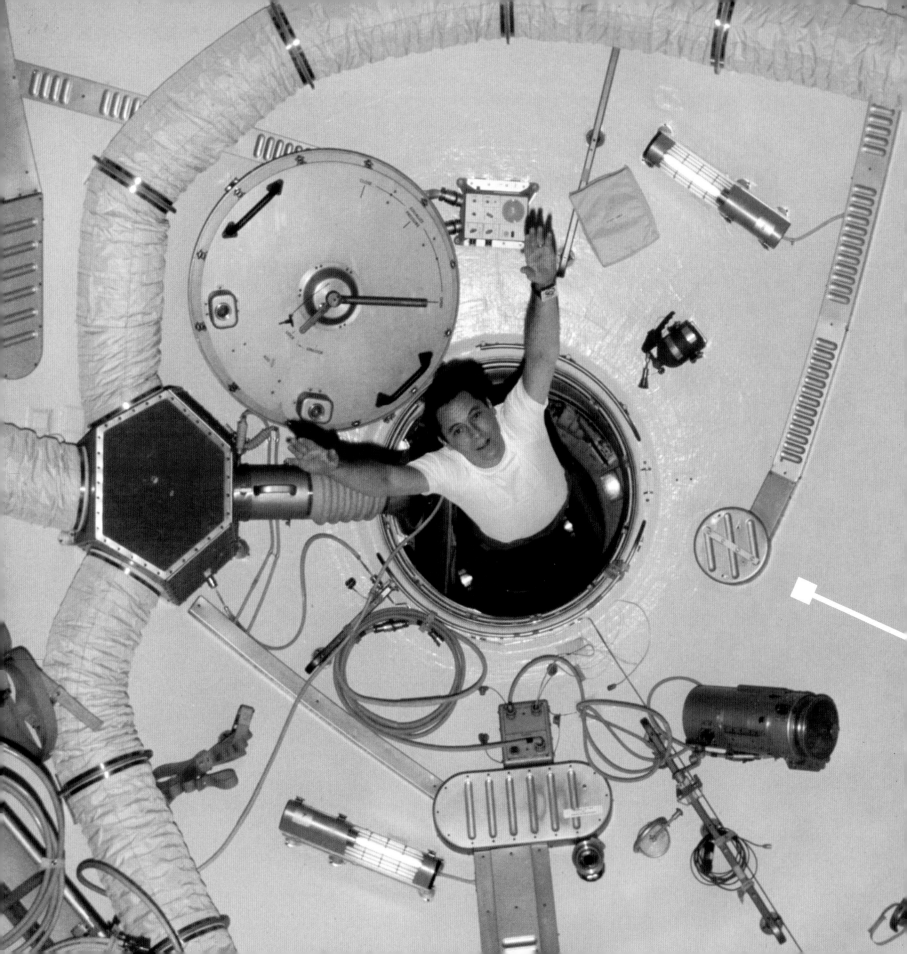

residents of the ISS are living in outer space, far above the Earth's surface. Who is up there? What are they doing? What is life like in outer space? How did the International Space Station come to be?

Astronaut and science pilot Edward Gibson floating inside the space station Skylab 4.

A HUMAN
GOES TO SPACE

The first human traveled to outer space on April 12, 1961. Yuri Gagarin, a Russian cosmonaut, flew a space capsule that exited Earth's atmosphere for 1 hour and 48 minutes. He made a single orbit, or revolution, around the world, and came back down.

As technology improved, the space programs in America and Russia started sending people up for longer and longer amounts of time. When America was sending Apollo spacecraft to the moon from 1968 to 1972, its astronauts were in space for up to 12 days.

After traveling to the moon, the Apollo spacecraft were used for another important mission: diplomacy. The United States and the Soviet Union had been great rivals, in both world politics and the space race. But in the 1970s, the two space programs started working together.

Scientists wanted space to be a place beyond the conflicts of Earth. When Neil Armstrong was on the moon, he told the then president Richard Nixon that "it is a great honor and privilege for us to be here representing not only the United States, but men of peaceable nations, men with an interest and a curiosity, and men with a vision for the future."

In 1975 the American Apollo spacecraft and the Russian Soyuz 19 were launched within a few hours of each other. The two space capsules met and docked in space. The astronauts and cosmonauts were together for two days, eating together, living together, and working together. As American astronaut Vance Brand later said, although their countries may have been rivals, "when you deal with people that are in the same line of work as you are, and you're around them for a short time, why, you discover that, well, they're human beings."

TOP: An artist's drawing of the American Apollo spacecraft docking with the Soviet Soyuz.

LEFT: Soviet cosmonaut Yuri Gagarin, the first man to go to space.

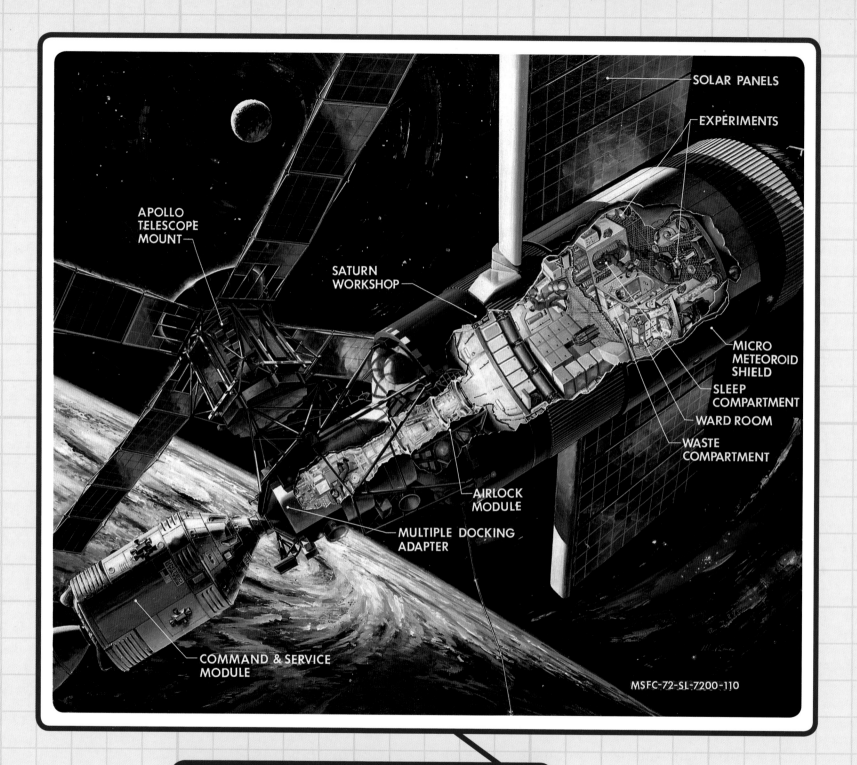

SOLAR PANELS

EXPERIMENTS

APOLLO
TELESCOPE
MOUNT

SATURN
WORKSHOP

MICRO
METEOROID
SHIELD

SLEEP
COMPARTMENT

WARD ROOM

WASTE
COMPARTMENT

AIRLOCK
MODULE

MULTIPLE DOCKING
ADAPTER

COMMAND & SERVICE
MODULE

MSFC-72-SL-7200-110

A look inside America's famous space station Skylab, which orbited the Earth 34,981 times before coming down in 1979.

A HUMBLE
BEGINNING

As technology got better, people started spending longer amounts of time in space. There was much to learn, such as how light behaves when it isn't in Earth's atmosphere, or what being in space does to the human body. So, the Soviet Union launched the first space station in 1971. It was called Salyut 1. The second crew to visit Salyut 1, made up of three cosmonauts, was in orbit for a record 24 days. But as they returned to Earth, the unspeakable happened. Their Soyuz capsule malfunctioned during reentry. Everyone aboard died as the capsule fell back to Earth. It was a tragic ending to such an important mission. The Salyut 1 space station was de-orbited, or removed from space, later that year.

The United States had problems with their first space station, too. When Skylab was launched in 1973, vibrations damaged its shielding. The first crew of astronauts to visit Skylab managed to fix the problems and get the station up and running. After 28 days in space, they returned to Earth. Two more missions aboard Skylab followed, each longer than the last.

As its name might tell you, Skylab was a great place to conduct scientific experiments. Astronauts watched spiders they had brought up with them. They were surprised to see the spiders made webs in space just as they did on Earth. This experiment proved that space was a place to which living creatures could adapt. The experiment was actually suggested by a high school student! When the astronauts returned to Earth, scientists studied how living in space had changed their bodies. Skylab eventually came back to Earth in 1979.

In the meantime, the Soviet Union launched and "de-orbited" another six Salyut space stations. And in 1986 the Russians launched the Mir space station. Mir was the largest, most advanced space station yet. It stayed in orbit for 15 years, until 2001. It was very international: over 100 people visited Mir, and only 40 were from Russia. Forty-four Americans spent time on Mir, as did six French astronauts, four Germans, and representatives from Great Britain, Japan, and other countries. American space shuttles visited Mir regularly—dropping off crew and supplies, and returning other crew members to Earth. Mir set the stage for the International Space Station.

A SPACE STATION
FOR ALL NATIONS

In the 1980s, NASA was making plans for a large space station. During the 1990s, however, those plans were changed to include other nations. With the help and knowledge of people in the Russian space program and others, the space station could be built faster and do more. Hence, it became known as the International Space Station.

Starting in 1998, it took 13 years and over 40 different shuttle and rocket launches to put the ISS together. Made of many different segments, the space station is 240 feet long and 357 feet across. It is bigger than a football field! It is the largest structure humans have ever put into space.

Fifteen different countries have contributed to the space station. The United States provided the main laboratory module, named Destiny. Scientific experiments are performed there. Canada provided the Canadarm, a robotic arm that was used to put the different segments together. It also moves payloads, or cargo, from space shuttles into place on the space station. It is still used to maintain the space station today. Russia adapted two modules from its designs for Mir 2: Zarya was the first ISS module that provided power, thrust, and guidance, and Zvezda became the first living quarters. Japan provided the Kibo module, which has an airlock for sending small satellites or other payloads into space. Italy built the Cupola, which is a valuable workspace. The Cupola also has the best views of Earth and visiting spacecraft.

The first Canadarm, seen here on space shuttle *Atlantis* in 2008, had a 30-year career with NASA. It moved massive payloads from the space shuttles into orbit. The Canadarm 2, a more advanced version, is on the ISS now.

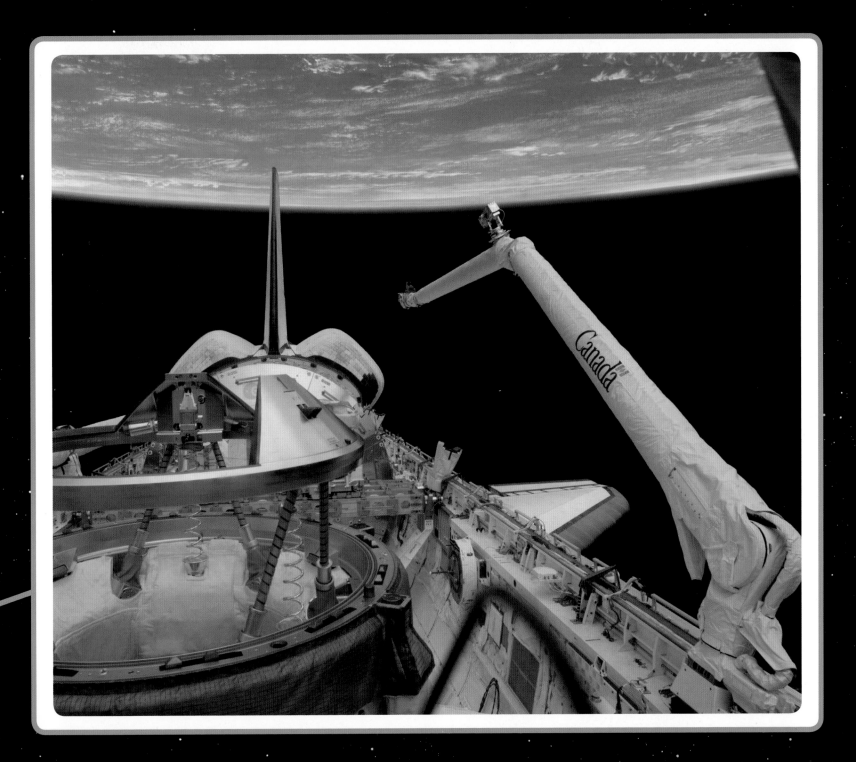

FROM TOP TO BOTTOM:
Charles Conrad Jr. enjoys a shower aboard Skylab.

LEFT SIDE: Gerald Carr balances his pilot William Pogue on his finger in Skylab's low-gravity environment.

LOWER, RIGHT: The stunning view of Earth from the Cupola on the International Space Station.

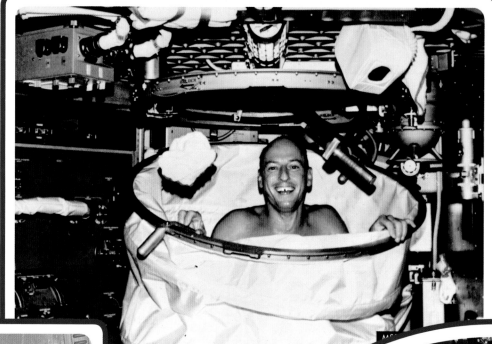

WHAT IS LIFE LIKE
ON THE ISS?

Humans on the ISS are the fastest people alive. Traveling at 17,500 miles per hour, they orbit the Earth every 90 minutes. They see the sun rise every hour and a half! They are also some of the hardest-working people. Altogether, the crew logs around 160 hours of research every week.

Even though they are living in space, people aboard the ISS try to have a normal life. They go into one of two small cabins to try to get the normal eight hours of sleep. They can sleep in a sleeping bag attached to the wall, but some people on the ISS prefer just to float around.

The ISS is considered a "low-gravity environment," which means that people on the space station float in the air, almost like how people on Earth float in water. It looks like a lot of fun, but living in a low-gravity environment can be hard. Crew members often feel sick to their stomach when they first arrive on the ISS. Without gravity's normal pull, blood gathers in their faces, making them look puffy, and some astronauts report that their noses always feel a little stuffed up. To give a sense of this feeling, NASA tests the effects of living in space by having people lie on beds that are uneven, with their feet slightly higher than their heads—something you can try at home!

Since their bodies are no longer fighting the full strength of Earth's gravity, crew members start to lose muscle strength and bone mass as well. Typically this only happens to the elderly here on Earth, but in a low-gravity environment, it happens to even the youngest and fittest astronauts. That is why it is important for crew members to exercise by running on a treadmill or pedaling an exercise bike. Still, coming back to Earth and its full gravity is hard on crew members after they have been in space a long time.

One of the long-term projects of the ISS is to test the physical and mental health effects of living in space. In a way, all of these researchers are themselves part of the research. Scientists hope to learn how to help people live more easily in low gravity, in preparation for longer trips farther into space.

WHO
GOES THERE?

People have been living on the ISS continuously since 2000. Starting in 2009, six-person crews have been regularly spending four to six months on the space station. But who are they, and what are they doing?

The space station is used for conducting research on space, so many of the crew members are scientists. Some are computer engineers. Some served in the military, and others have backgrounds in medicine. Still others are teachers.

For example, Takuya Onishi worked as an airline pilot in Japan before training to become a flight engineer on the ISS in 2016. Kathleen Rubins earned a doctorate in cancer biology and studied diseases before becoming an astronaut and going to the ISS. She became the first person to sequence DNA in space.

Everyone NASA sends to the space station undergoes astronaut training. The training takes one to two years in Houston, Texas. There, future astronauts learn how the ISS works and are exposed to what they may experience on board the space station. Because communication with the ground and with other astronauts is important, astronauts must also learn to understand Russian. They study the ISS's electrical, heating and cooling, and communications systems, so they can operate them in case of emergencies. Gravity is different on the ISS, so astronauts learn to function in low gravity by training underwater on Earth. They also prepare for emergencies and accidents that may occur both in space or when the crew is in the process of returning to Earth, such as landing in the jungle.

Life on the ISS means doing science experiments and also your exercises—but astronauts find time for fun too.

"Sitting down to a meal" while you're in orbit doesn't involve much "sitting down" at all!

EATING AND DRINKING
ON THE ISS

Microgravity changes how people eat and drink. We don't think too much about everything that gravity does, but imagine trying to drink a glass of water while the water keeps floating away! Imagine eating a plate of spaghetti when the noodles won't stay still!

In the early days of space flight, living in microgravity meant that astronauts and cosmonauts ate only cold food paste from aluminum tubes or little cubes. Crew members weren't in space very long, but it seems like something you'd get tired of. So, on the ISS, astronauts get to choose from over 100 foods. They pick a menu before they go to space and have plenty of snacks and fresh fruit. There's even salt and pepper, although to keep the granules from floating all over the place, the spices are in liquid form.

Normal human functions can be difficult when you're orbiting the Earth. Since you can't even sit down in space without floating out of a chair, the toilet on the ISS has toe clips that crew members slip their feet into. To keep the air in the space station clean, there is a fan that creates suction, like a vacuum cleaner, which takes the waste away. Solid waste is stored in bags and is eventually cast off in capsules that burn up in the atmosphere. Liquid waste is collected and carefully purified, becoming water again for crew members to drink. That sounds gross, but the water is safe and clean, and the process is much easier than transporting a lot of heavy water up to the ISS.

Because water is so precious, astronauts don't take showers while they are on the ISS. Instead they wash up with a damp, soapy cloth. On Skylab, showers could take two hours! It took up too much space and wasn't really worth it. Astronauts only change their clothes every three days on the ISS. Their worn clothes get put into a special capsule and burn up during reentry to Earth.

HOW TO SHOP
FOR THE ISS

When the International Space Station was being built, many of the modules came up on board NASA's space shuttle. Space shuttles were sort of like the trucks of space, and they brought crews and equipment to the ISS until 2011.

Space shuttles weren't designed to be used forever. In 2003, the space shuttle *Columbia* tragically disintegrated as it was returning to Earth, killing all seven astronauts on board. It was clear that the shuttle program had to end. But the shuttles were so necessary for the ISS that they were used for another eight years. The final shuttle mission, flown by the shuttle *Atlantis*, was a short trip to the ISS to drop off more equipment.

After the shuttle program stopped, though, there wasn't another good replacement ready to bring supplies to ISS. So the ISS program turned to an even older vessel: the Soyuz capsule. Crews of three ride up in a Soyuz capsule. It takes about six hours to get from the launch site in Baikonur, Kazakhstan, to the ISS.

The Soyuz is the only capsule that people still travel in, but the ISS gets supplies via other spacecraft. The Russian spacecraft Progress has proven to be a reliable way to get supplies to the space station without the need of a crew. The United States sends up supplies in Cygnus capsules on top of Atlas V rockets. The European Space Agency and the Japanese Aerospace Exploration Agency have also made unmanned deliveries.

Nowadays other space programs that aren't run by governments are getting into the game, too. A company called Space X has sent scientific equipment, small satellites, and other things to the ISS using their Dragon capsules. NASA especially likes working with these capsules, because the Dragon can also carry things back down to Earth, such as equipment from completed experiments or blood samples from astronauts.

Companies like Space X and Blue Origin, which was started by the man who founded Amazon.com, are working on rockets that will be able to deliver people to the ISS as well. If you go to space, maybe you'll ride in one of them.

The space shuttle *Atlantis* launching from John F. Kennedy Space Center in Florida.

American businessman Dennis Tito on the left poses with cosmonauts Talgat Musabayev and Yuri Baturin aboard the ISS in 2001.

SO, YOU WANT TO VISIT?

The famous international space station seems like a cool place to live and work, but people who aren't scientists have made the trip just to visit.

In April 2001, a businessman named Dennis Tito rode a Soyuz spacecraft up to the space station. He was the first person to pay to go into space as a tourist, and he stayed on board for six days. Tito wanted to go to into space for 40 years, ever since he heard about Yuri Gagarin's first flight. He had even worked as an engineer at NASA's Jet Propulsion Laboratory before working in finance. He made a lot of money in business, which is good, because going to space is expensive—people estimate Tito paid as much as 20 million dollars.

Today, it costs 45 to 50 million dollars for a trip to the ISS. Even though it costs a lot, people are willing to pay for the unique privilege of visiting the ISS. Since Dennis Tito's flight, six more people have paid to visit the ISS. All of them are very wealthy.

But after the shuttle program was halted and the Soyuz became the only way to get to and from orbit, space tourism was paused. Space tourism may get going again soon. The company Blue Origin wants to start letting people pay to go into space by 2018. The company has said that people won't be going as far as the ISS at first. They'll be taking shorter, suborbital flights, where passengers will experience microgravity for three to six minutes. As the technology develops and becomes more popular, it seems likely that the cost will come down. Would you like to visit space? You could take selfies with Earth, do endless space flips, and see stars more clearly than you can imagine.

SPACEWALKING

One of the coolest jobs on the International Space Station is getting to put on a spacesuit and go outside on a spacewalk. The first person ever to spacewalk was the Russian cosmonaut Alexei Leonov. On March 18, 1965, he left his Voskhod capsule for 10 minutes.

On the ISS, people who go on spacewalks are usually outside for five to eight hours. They go out to perform maintenance on the ISS or on other satellites. Some spacewalks are used to conduct scientific experiments.

To survive in space, astronauts have to wear large spacesuits. The suits provide them with air and keep their bodies warm. Astronauts put on their spacesuits hours before the spacewalk. They start breathing pure oxygen to lower the amount of nitrogen in their blood. While the nitrogen in the air we breathe is normally not a problem, the lower pressure in spacesuits could allow painful nitrogen bubbles to form inside astronauts' blood.

After several hours breathing pure oxygen, astronauts go out into space. Usually they go out in pairs. They stay attached to the space station with a steel tether that is very strong—able to hold up to 1,100 pounds without breaking apart. It's never happened, but if the tether should fail, astronauts can use something like a jet pack, which they wear, to get back. They can steer their way using a joystick. It sounds like a video game, and in fact, video games are one way that astronauts prepare for the spacewalks. When on Earth, they also practice wearing the spacesuits underwater.

Although astronauts aren't worried about floating away, there are some dangers to being in space. In 2013 a problem with Italian astronaut Luca Parmitano's spacesuit caused his water supply to start leaking into his helmet. He was in danger of drowning in space! Parmitano kept his cool and made it back to the airlock.

Sometimes the Canadarm is used to move astronauts around. In 2010, Stephen Bowen was attached to the Canadarm during a spacewalk. Suddenly the Canadarm stopped responding. Bowen was stuck! The astronauts inside the space station were able to figure out that it was a software problem. It was just a little hiccup in his spacewalk that lasted more than six hours.

In the top right picture, astronauts prepare for spacewalks by training underwater. In the bottom left, you can see a spacewalk in action.

WHERE DO WE GO FROM HERE?

The International Space Station is a place for scientific experiments, but in a way, the station itself is an experiment. How do you build and maintain a space station in low Earth orbit? The ISS has been preparing us for the next step into space. But what is that next step? And what will happen to the ISS when we are done with it?

President Barack Obama renewed the lease on the ISS through 2024. With the support of the United States, the ISS will last until then.

The work that has been done on the space station has been great preparation for the next steps that NASA wants to take: retrieving and studying an asteroid in the 2020s, and sending people to Mars in the 2030s. We've learned how being in space affects the human body, and we've practiced assembling a spacecraft while in orbit.

Scientists believe whenever we do start sending people deeper into space, their spacecraft will probably be assembled in orbit as the ISS was. Space stations could be sort of like airports, where spacecraft can fuel up and pick up passengers and supplies on their way to the moon, Mars, or elsewhere.

When the ISS is eventually retired, probably in the 2020s, it will have played a valuable role in whatever comes next. Who knows? Maybe someday you will be bouncing on Mars, leading a team of astronauts. If so, you would have the ISS to thank.

MARS
EXPLORERS WANTED

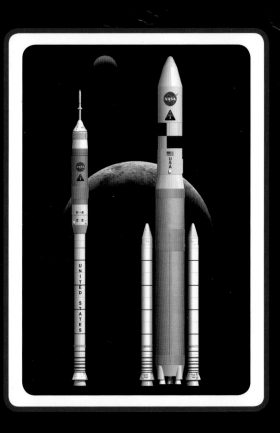

Though people haven't visited yet, NASA's Ares rockets were designed to eventually put humans on the planet.

MEET THE EXPERT

MICHAEL SHARA, Curator, Department of Astrophysics
American Museum of Natural History, New York City

Dr. Michael Shara is Curator in the Department of Astrophysics at the American Museum of Natural History. He produces space shows and exhibitions seen by millions of visitors every year. He also leads a team of research astrophysicists that studies the structure and evolution of novae and supernovae and the populations of stars inhabiting star clusters and galaxies. Prior to joining the Museum, he was with the Space Telescope Science Institute at Johns Hopkins University for 17 years where he was responsible for the peer review committees for the Hubble Space Telescope. He is also adjunct professor of Astronomy at Columbia University. Dr. Shara frequently observes with the Hubble Space Telescope and other large ground-based telescopes. In his spare time he is a gung-ho scuba diver enjoying the company of sharks in the South Pacific.

Index